Fruits of the Earth

The CAFOD/DLT Lent Book 2002

Reflections on the

Joseph Donders ✦ Jeanne Hinton
Jayne Hoose ✦ Matthew Kukah
Oliver McTernan ✦ Margaret Silf

Fruits of the Earth

Reflections on the
Scripture Readings for Lent 2002

DARTON · LONGMAN + TODD

First published in Great Britain in 2001 by
CAFOD
Romero Close
Stockwell Road
London SW9 9TY

Darton, Longman and Todd Ltd
Spencer Court
140-142 Wandsworth High Street
London SW18 4JJ

ISBN 0 232 52443 2

Cover photo: Pieternella Pieterse
Design: Garry Lambert

Bible quotations are taken predominantly from the New
Jerusalem Bible, published and copyright © 1985 by Darton,
Longman and Todd Ltd and Doubleday and Co Inc.

Printed and bound in Great Britain by Page Bros,
Norwich, Norfolk

Contents

About the authors

Joseph Donders teaches and lectures worldwide. His many books include *Praying and Preaching the Sunday Gospel* and *The Fullness of Time*.

Jeanne Hinton is a writer and helps lead workshops on 'a new way of being church'.

Jayne Hoose is a writer in Christian ethics and development and a regional organiser for CAFOD.

Matthew Kukah is the former General Secretary to the Nigerian Bishops' Conference.

Oliver McTernan is a broadcaster and writer, currently working at the Weatherhead Center for International Affairs, Harvard.

Margaret Silf is a writer and retreat-giver. Her books include *Wayfaring*, *Landmarks* and *Taste and See*.

Introduction

Although we are hardly the first to think it, it is difficult not to feel that we are living at a special moment in history.

As these reflections on the church's chosen readings for Lent show, our preparation for Easter shadows the wilderness experience of Jesus. For Christians, this was the moment when the whole of creation was poised between two futures. For the first followers of Jesus Lent was the time when candidates for baptism prepared themselves to change their lives forever. And for Christians today it is also a special time of expectancy, reflection and making choices. We ask ourselves, Who do we want to be? What values are we to live by? What do we hope for? Who we are to follow?

The extraordinary promise and power of the gospel lies in its message that our own personal story is one small but precious fragment in the story of creation. The future is always fragile, difficult and uncertain. Each moment offers a new beginning, the chance to start afresh. The past, and all its mistakes, is in God's hands. What matters is how we answer the question, 'What happens next?' As Margaret Silf writes in her reflection on the readings for the Thursday after Ash Wednesday, 'Just a faint touch on the rudder of our lives – a tweak away from the partialness of "self" towards the wholeness of God and God's creation – has the potential to turn the world's "ship" in the direction of God's own justice, peace and love.'

'Lent', as Oliver McTernan reminds us, 'is our opportunity to release the power of God's compassion into a world that stands in much need of it.' Throughout history men and women, often men and women who had previously struggled to find a voice, have found in these readings and others like them the vision and the strength to claim a different future for themselves and their children. In their experience of God the dispossessed, the exploited and the disregarded have discovered in themselves an authority to speak the truth in love. Each person is equally precious in the sight of God, and the earth and its fruits have been entrusted to us to share.

Where there is self-righteousness and certainty we can bring only humility and the recognition of our own faults and failings. Where there is despair we can bring only a stubborn resolve to reach for a future beyond violence and resentment, where, in the words of Seamus Heaney, 'hope and history rhyme'.

Brendan Walsh

Margaret Silf
Ash Wednesday to Saturday after Ash Wednesday

Ash Wednesday

Undercover agents

Jl 2: 12-18; Ps 50; Co 5: 20 - 6:2; Mt 6: 1-6, 16-18

'When you pray, go to your private room and, when you have shut your door, pray to your Father who is in that secret place, and your Father who sees all that is done in secret will reward you.'

(Matthew 6:6)

There was a bit of a stand-off among the folk of St Jude's. The church was in a deprived neighbourhood, bristling with every kind of need. A Christian presence in that place, if it was to be true to the Gospel, surely had to be doing something to combat the despair and dereliction of the people on its doorstep.

'We should be getting on with things,' some people clamoured, 'not just sitting here praying.' Others, meanwhile, quietly went on praying. 'We can't do a thing about it on our own,' they said. 'All we can do is ask God to do something.' There was stalemate.

Is it really 'either/or'? Or might this time of reflection in the weeks of Lent be an opportunity to embrace the 'both/and' of contemplation and action? A time to reflect on the need not only to expend energy on addressing the pressing needs of our time and place, but also to draw on the source of that energy, which is God?

This dynamic of receiving and giving, drawing on and expending, is everywhere in evidence. Our bodies insist on the restoration of sleep in readiness for the challenges of the coming day. In winter the trees direct their energy to the tap root to draw on the secret energy of the earth that will make possible the explosion of springtime. And Jesus himself, in whose name we long to be 'active', consistently withdrew into the 'secret place of prayer', to draw from his Father the resources he needed to live out the True Life on planet Earth.

Prayer, in all its apparent passivity, is the powerhouse of all our 'doing', not an optional extra to be fitted in when there is a bit of slack.

But prayer has a life of its own. It won't let itself be confined by our fences or programmed into our flowcharts. To pray is to engage in subversive activity – to bring God into our human dealings. No doubt the child Jesus was taught to put on his prayer shawl and go to the Father. We do the same, figuratively, when we withdraw into the 'secret place' of our prayer. We become 'undercover agents', concealed in solitude, hidden in the blanket of God's stillness, called both to listen to God in that darkness and to live out what we have heard, in the full light of day.

Thought for the day
The cloak of solitude and silence that enfolds us in prayer is like the shell of an egg in which our part of Christ's Kingdom is growing and coming to birth.

Prayer
Lord,
forgive our foolish hearts,
that want the chicken without the egg or the egg without the chicken.
Grow your Kingdom in the darkness of our prayer
and bring it to the light of day in our passionate living of the True Life in you.
Amen.

Thursday after Ash Wednesday

The shape of your cross

Dt 30: 15-20; Ps 1; Lk 9: 22-25

'If anyone wants to be a follower of mine, let him renounce himself and take up his cross every day and follow me.'

(Luke 9: 23)

I hope I'm not the only Christian to have thrown the reproach at God: 'It's all very well for *you*, Lord – you were never a woman, a parent, unemployed, old and infirm ...'

Jesus of Nazareth lived amid one particular set of circumstances, through a few short years, in a specific Middle Eastern culture. But the Christian process of redemption that begins with Jesus of Nazareth, the Alpha point, leads right through to the fullness of the Kingdom, the cosmic Christ, the Omega point.

So God can – and *does* – respond to my querulous complaining with a straightforward answer: 'No, I was never a married woman, the parent of teenagers, or a carer of infirm parents – *but I am now*, because these are precisely the circumstances I am living out, and redeeming, in your life, here and now, in the place where you find yourself.'

When God reminds me that my own circumstances, however unwelcome, are part of *his* place of being human in the twenty-first century, I begin to feel a bit differently about 'picking up my cross and following him'. My life's situations and dilemmas are not so much things to be endured, ignored, or patched up with band-aid. They are a unique pathway through life that can become a redemptive pathway for all creation, if I am willing to live it alongside the Lord.

Seen in this light, 'renouncing myself' is far from being a command to live somehow as though I wasn't there. Rather, it becomes an invitation to re-set my inner compass, so that I discern every next step not by wondering, 'What suits me best, makes me happy, avoids my pain?' but by asking, 'In this situation, what is the more loving, the more Christ-like way to respond?'

This change of focus is something we can begin to practise day by day in our personal choices and decisions. Just a faint touch on the rudder of our lives – a tweak away from the partialness of 'self' towards the wholeness of God and God's creation – has the potential to turn the world's 'ship' in the direction of God's own justice, peace and love.

Thought for the day

Reflect on your own specific and immediate circumstances. What is dominating your energies right now? Whatever it is – illness, problems at work, or an unhappy love affair – turn it into this thought: 'Right now, in my personal circumstances, Christ is redeeming what it means to be ill, or exploited at work, or in an unhappy relationship.'

Prayer

Lord,
you desire every possible human situation to be redeemed.
Give me the grace to recognise what you are redeeming in my own situation right now,
and the courage to let you live it and redeem it
in and through my choices, decisions and reactions.

Amen.

Friday after Ash Wednesday

Washing both feet

Is 58: 1-9; Ps 50; Mt 9: 14-15

'Why should we fast if you never see it,
why do penance if you never notice?'

(Isaiah 58: 3)

A friend of mine was waiting to collect her son, who had an appointment at the doctor's surgery after school. 'Nothing serious, I hope,' I commented lightly. 'Oh no,' she replied. 'Just a rash on his foot, but I want the doctor to have a look at it.'

The next day I asked her how the visit had gone. She started to chuckle. 'Before we went I sent him to the bathroom to wash his feet,' she said. 'He came out with one foot washed and the other still ensconced in a sweaty sock. I couldn't believe it. "You've only washed one foot!" "But Mum," he replied, "I've only got a rash on one foot."'

At first I thought only a child can operate that kind of logic – 'If the doctor won't see it, why wash it?' But when I tune into to the inner workings of my own mind I find similar little conversations going on all the time: 'I don't want to do this, but I'd better, because people may notice if I don't', or, 'I can't be bothered doing this, and no-one is looking, so there's no need to make the effort.'

So what is my real motivation I wonder? Frighteningly often I come to the conclusion that my choices have been made in the service of my own need of affirmation and approval, or my own desire for an easy life.

Lent calls us to a radical spring clean of these subtle motivations. It challenges us to 'wash both feet', regardless of whether the doctor examines them or not. Our *whole* self needs cleansing of its me-centred motives if we are to grow into people who are truly Christ-centred.

Isaiah goes on to spell out the kind of spiritual schizophrenia that follows if we insist on staying with our 'If you don't see it, it ain't there' attitude. The seeds of every kind of hypocrisy lurk in this dislocation of our visible behaviour and our invisible motives. 'Integrity' follows when we dare to look at them both together, and take the pain of bringing them back into line with each other.

Thought for the day
A woman drove through the middle of a busy city one night with her friend. When they got home, the friend said: 'Do you realise that you've been driving without any lights?' 'It doesn't matter', the driver excused herself, 'Nobody saw me!'

Prayer
Lord,
give me the grace to 'love the me I hide' enough to risk bringing her to you,
just as she is,
for your cleansing and healing.

Amen.

Saturday after Ash Wednesday

Precious stones among the rubble

Is 58: 9-14; Ps 85: 1-6; Lk 5: 27-32

'You will rebuild the ancient ruins, you will build upon an old foundation. You will be called "Breach-Mender", "Restorer of ruined houses" .'

(Isaiah 58: 12)

In the city of Dresden in the former East Germany, the Frauenkirche is being restored. Along with the rest of the city and many of its hapless citizens, the Frauenkirche was destroyed on the night of 13 February 1945 by enemy bombardment. This act of apparently wanton destruction left a running abscess of suspicion, hatred and desire for revenge.

I visited Dresden a couple of years ago and sought out the Frauenkirche. What I found took me by surprise. In the square in front of what had been the main façade of the magnificent cathedral church there were rows and rows of shelves, where every stone that could be salvaged from the ruins was stored and numbered. Each stone was carefully cherished, waiting to be incorporated into the new, restored church.

Some of the old stones are quite beyond repair or too brittle to use. They reminded me of some of the attitudes that pervade our ways of being church and of being human. Some have crumbled into disrepute and must be let go. Some have become bulky blockages, obstructions to renewal. It takes prayerful discernment to distinguish between what is furthering the growth of new vision and direction, and what is militating against it.

As individuals, too, we each have our brittle bits and our hard knots of obstructiveness. But the market place in Dresden gives me an assurance that we also have a 'true self', a living core within us, known, numbered, cherished, and etched on the palm of God's hand. We may feel that we are simply 'on the shelf', like those rows and rows of salvaged stones in Dresden, but the Master Builder has a place for us.

The restoration of the Frauenkirche is a fine and ambitious project. But the restored church will not just be a replica of the one that was destroyed. The new church will be a new creation. It is being built in a new spirit of reconciliation, repentance, grief, and a longing for a new order. It is being built by craftsmen, artists and sculptors from many different nations and of all faiths and denominations.

It helps me to trust that the Kingdom of God, too, is being shaped and fashioned out of our broken pieces, that in that Kingdom there is room both for those who are broken and for those who did the breaking, and that this Kingdom will be at once the re-making of the old, and the making of something unimaginably new.

Thought for the day
Our worst wrong-doings can be re-shaped into new beginnings, if we let God be the Builder.

Prayer
Lord,
as we wander disconsolately through what we see as the rubble of our lives
please open our eyes to see the diamonds among the stones and turn us into co-workers in your great project of re-creation.

Amen.

Margaret Silf
First week of Lent

First Sunday of Lent

The Great Untruth

Gn 2: 7-9, 3: 1-7; Ps 50; Rm 5: 12-19; Mt 4: 1-11

Then the serpent said to the woman, 'God knows in fact that on the day you eat (from the forbidden tree) your eyes will be opened and you will be like gods, knowing good and evil.'

(Genesis 3: 4-5)

There is a delightful vignette in the story of the Fall, as told in Genesis, of God making tunics for his fallen creatures to protect them from the consequences of their folly. I can remember when this touching image was first pointed out to me by a wise friend, who liked to imagine God peering over his pince-nez, needle in hand, stitching animal skins together for two disobedient children.

Today's text, of course, pre-dates all that. The Fall is still to come, and instead of the thread of God's love re-weaving a broken creation we see the thick coil of the serpent threading his way through the lush long grass of Eden, searching for a place to begin the unravelling of God's Dream.

The serpent's slick words are the overture to the Great Untruth. We need some translation here because we have almost forgotten what Truth sounds like. And so 'Eat and be filled' is actually a sentence to be hungry for ever. 'Having your eyes opened' turns out to be the quickest route to inner blindness. And 'Becoming like gods' in practice leads us to lose touch almost completely with the God within and around us.

From now on everything we say and do and think and feel, far from being the truth about ourselves, may be an inversion of that truth, the Big Deception. When we feel full of so much that we cherish, we may be at our most empty. What we think we see most clearly may be the most dangerous of illusions. Our imagined certainties may be quicksands and our demons may come disguised as angels of light.

Until, eventually, we become capable of letting millions starve around us yet sense no injustice. We watch television reports of massacres of thousands of people, yet see no evil. We tell ourselves that we know God, yet fail to recognise him in our neighbour.

Whose side are we on? Will we join forces with the Great Untruth, and rest easy in our illusions, offering the serpent a place to do his unravelling? Or will we commit ourselves to the God who is still weaving his Dream back together from the broken threads of our lives and our world.

Thought for the day
Co-weaver, or Unraveller of God's Dream – which way will my actions be directed today?

Prayer
Just for today,
may I choose the ways of the Weaver,
follow the paths of Truth
and cherish the Becoming of God's Dream
in everything I think, and say, and do.
Amen.

First Monday of Lent

A sandwich for supper

Lv 19: 1-2, 11-18; Ps 18; Mt 25: 31-46

*'Go away from me, with my curse upon you ... for I was
hungry and you never gave me food; I was thirsty and
you never gave me anything to drink; I was a stranger
and you never made me welcome; naked and you never
clothed me; sick and in prison and you never visited me.'*

(Matthew 25: 41-44)

A story tells of a man who went to the office every day in
his expensive car, and made important decisions and
signed big contracts. When this important man enjoyed
business lunches he would try to distract the attention of
his influential guests from the unsavoury spectacle of the
beggars on the streets of his city.

One evening after a hard day making money he packed his
briefcase to go home, where supper would be waiting for
him. As he was locking his desk for the night he caught
sight of a stale sandwich lying abandoned at the back of
the drawer. Without much thought he crammed it in his
coat pocket. No need for it to go mouldy and mess up his
desk. On the way out to the car park he saw a beggar on
the steps, huddled in an old blanket. 'Here, my friend,' he
said to the beggar. 'Here is something for your supper.'
And he gave him the stale sandwich.

That night the man dreamed that he was away on a
business trip. After the day's meeting, he was taken with
his fellow directors to the town's most luxurious restaurant.
Everyone gave their orders, and settled down with their
aperitifs to look forward to a convivial evening.

The orders arrived. Pate de fois gras. Medallions of venison. Lamb cutlets with rosemary and garlic. The dishes being brought to the table brought gasps of delight from all the company. Then his own order appeared. A waitress set in front of him one small plate, on which was served ... a stale sandwich!

'What kind of service is this?' the man demanded, enraged. 'This isn't what I ordered! I thought this was the best restaurant in town!'

'Oh sir,' the waitress told him. 'You've been misinformed. This isn't a restaurant at all. This is heaven. We are only able to serve you what you have sent on ahead while you were alive. I'm very sorry, sir, but when we looked under your name, the best we could find to serve to you was this little sandwich.'

(Adapted from a Jewish folk tale.)

Thought for the day
The next person you meet is Jesus in disguise.

Prayer
Lord,
please give us eyes to see you in each other
and to act on what we see.

Amen.

A rolling coin gathers a lot of love

Is 55: 10-11; Ps 33; Mt 6: 7-15

'As the rain and the snow come down from the heavens and do not return without watering the earth, making it yield and giving growth to provide seed for the sower and bread for the eating, so the word that goes from my mouth does not return to me empty, without carrying out my will and succeeding in what it was sent to do.'

(Isaiah 55: 10-11)

An old story tells of a wise old man, who owned a precious golden coin. One day as he sat gazing at this precious coin and rejoicing in its beauty a thought occurred to him. 'It isn't right that I should be the only person to have the pleasure of possessing this golden coin. What use is it, if no-one shares it?' And he went out and gave the coin to a passing child.

The child couldn't believe her luck. She couldn't take her eyes off this shining coin. Then she had a sudden idea: 'I'll give this coin to Mum. She needs so many things. This coin will make her very happy.'

Of course, the child's mother was delighted with the coin – such an unexpected solution to so many of her problems. She pondered in her mind as to how to spend it and what to buy first.

As she was thinking about this there was a knock at the door, and there stood a street beggar. 'Poor soul,' she thought. 'He has nothing, and we are just about getting by.' And she gave the gold coin to the beggar.

The beggar was speechless. This coin could be turned into food for a month. He made his way back to the subway where he slept, and there he noticed a new resident, just arrived. The poor man was blind and crippled. No chance of getting anywhere near to the folks who might have spared him a coin or two.

'I guess he needs it more than I do,' he thought to himself. And he pressed the gold coin into the blind man's thin, cold fingers.

That evening a wise old man walked through the dark subway. He noticed the blind, crippled beggar and stopped to speak to him. The beggar couldn't remember the last time anyone had bothered to speak to him.

After a while, the wise old man put his arm round the beggar's shoulder. 'I've nothing left to give you, except my friendship,' he murmured.

A tear rolled across the cheek of the blind beggar. How could he ever repay this gift of human kindness that had changed a dark night into a new dawn? With his shaking, aching hands, he reached into his pocket, brought out the golden coin and gave it to his new-found friend.

'Thank you for loving me,' he said.

(Loosely based on a story by Karl Tilke.)

Thought for the day
The coin of our loving will return to us, leaving seeds of joy all along its route – but only if we first give it away.

Prayer
Lord,
please give us the grace to give the best of ourselves away
with a free hand and a free heart,
in the way you yourself have taught us.

Amen.

First Wednesday of Lent

All breakages must be paid for

Jon 3: 1-10; Ps 50; Lk 11: 29-32

'Men and beasts, herds and flocks, are to taste nothing;
they must not eat, they must not drink water. All are to
put on sackcloth and call on God with all their might.'

(Jonah 3: 7-8)

Nineveh has been behaving badly, and Jonah, reluctant messenger for God, has warned its citizens of God's impending anger. The king has taken flight and called the whole city to order. 'God is angry, and not without cause,' he proclaims. 'We are all involved in this – man, woman, child and beast. The evil we have done has infected everything, and every living thing must pay the price.'

And so we have the slightly quaint spectacle of the King of Nineveh calling for a universal fast. No exemptions on grounds of extreme age or extreme youth. It's an all-or-nothing matter now, and even the flocks and herds are to abstain from food and drink.

A quaint spectacle? But also a spectacle that is re-enacted in so many ways in the pages of our daily newspapers and the images on our television screens. Because the facts are stark and uncompromising: what we as grown men and women get so badly wrong, our children, our animals, all living things and the earth itself have to pay for.

The story of Nineveh is ours today. Our determination to buy our food as cheaply as we can but to sell our products for the highest possible price has opened the Pandora's Box of contaminated food chains and resistant disease. Our expectation that we can drive our cars on demand and jet at will around the globe has seduced us into risking nature's revenge in storms and floods, devastating the land and decimating its creatures. Our refusal to live in right relationship with each other has condemned the young and the old to crippling isolation. And our insistence on defending the indefensible has stored up armouries of hell, ready to be hurled in any direction that is perceived as posing a threat to our security.

The only difference between ourselves and Nineveh is that we are still looking for a King who will make us wake up to the facts, and take steps to turn the tide of destruction before the earth and its creatures pay the ultimate penalty.

Thought for the day

The King who makes the difference is waiting to be invited in. Dare we listen to the challenge of his message? All creation waits for our reply.

Prayer

Lord of all creation,
your sheep and your cattle,
your dolphins and your butterflies,
your rivers and your valleys,
all cry out to us for mercy.
Open our ears to hear their desperate pleading,
before darkness falls.

Amen.

God's hands are at the end of our arms

Est 4: 1-3, 5: 12-14; Ps 137; Mt 7: 7-12

'You stretch out your hand and save me,
Your hand will do all things for me'

(Psalm 137: 7)

A story tells how a man wandered through a forest and came across an injured fox. The poor creature had been pursued by the huntsmen and had broken its legs in its efforts to escape. Now it lay in the undergrowth, helpless to find food.

The man's heart went out to the fox, but as he watched, a grizzly bear loomed up out of the trees, dragging the carcase of an animal it had killed. The bear appeared to ignore the presence of the wounded fox, but when he shuffled off again after his meal, he left the remains of the carcase close to where the fox was hiding.

The fox devoured the meat avidly.

The next day the man walked through the forest again. Again the bear left a tasty morsel behind for the hungry fox. And the third day the same thing happened.

The man pondered hard over what he had seen. 'If God cares so much for a wounded fox,' he thought, 'how much more will he care for me. My faith is far too feeble. I must learn to trust in God as this fox trusts.'

So the man went into a quiet corner of the forest and prayed: 'Loving Father, this injured fox has shown me what it means to trust you. Now I too commit myself entirely to your care. I trust that you will care for me just as you care for the fox.' And with this, he lay down and waited for God to act.

A day passed, and nothing happened. The man was getting hungry. A second day passed and still nothing happened. The man was deeply puzzled. A third day passed, and the man was angry. 'Father,' he cried, 'you love that little fox more than you love me! Why won't you care for me when I trust you so much? Why don't you feed me?'

At last, hunger forced him back into the town. There on the streets the man came upon a starving child. He railed on God in his rage. 'Why don't you do something?'

'I have done something,' God said. 'I have created you. But you choose to behave like the fox when you could model yourself on the bear.'

(Adapted from a fable by the Arabian mystic Sa'di.)

Thought for the day
Trustful contemplation becomes real when it leads to compassionate action.

Prayer
Lord,
your desire to do all things for us
asks the loan of our hands
to make your Dream a reality.
Give us the grace to put our hands
as well as our hearts
at your service.
Amen.

First Friday of Lent

Wake-up call

Ez 18: 21-28; Ps 129; Mt 5: 20-26

*'My soul is longing for the Lord
more than watchmen for daybreak'*

(Psalm 129: 6)

To pray for peace in a world that constantly puts itself through the shredder of war, or for justice in a market place that is fuelled by greed, sometimes seems pointless, a bad joke.

I ran up against the same kind of helplessness during the last weeks of my mother's losing battle against cancer. During those weeks I would sit with her through the dark watches of long, empty nights, until the morphine blessed her with a few hours of unconsciousness, as the dawn drew close.

I learned something of what it means to 'watch for daybreak'.

I also learned something I hadn't known before – that before the dawn chorus proper begins, there is a solitary birdsong. I still don't know which bird it was, whose morning exsultet broke the grip of the night. It always happened some short time before the full supporting orchestra of a July dawn chorus tuned up. I began to long for that solitary note. It meant that another day was dawning. There was going to be light again, at the end of another long dark tunnel of pain.

Some years later I came across these words:

'Faith is the bird who sings while night is still dark.'

I remembered the bird who had been my sole companion in those pre-dawn hours at my mother's bedside. I had learned to trust that birdsong. It spoke to me of a real promise of light in a place that was still deeply dark. And it was also a call to the entire bird world to wake up to the new day.

It helps me to trust that the 'pointless' prayer for peace amid war, for justice amid oppression, for hope amid despair, is not as futile as it often seems.

Such prayer can light a single candle, and that single candle can bring just enough light to enable many others to find their own candles and liberate a blaze to light up the whole of creation.

Thought for the day

A single pure note of prayer is all it takes to break the silence of hopelessness.

Prayer

Thank you, Lord,
for the bird who dares to sing while it is still dark,
and for those who dare to keep on praying when the clouds are down.
Please give us the grace to respond to the wake-up call
and sing out the fullness of our longing for peace and justice and hope –
loud enough to awaken an indifferent world.
Amen.

A 'fair' deal, or a just world?

Dt 26:16-19; Ps 118; Mt 5:43-48

'I say this to you: love your enemies and pray for those who persecute you; in this way you will be sons of your Father in heaven, for he causes the sun to rise on bad men as well as good, and his rain to fall on honest and dishonest alike.'

(Matthew 5: 44-45)

'It's not fair' I used to complain, like most small children, every time creation failed to serve my immediate requirements. To which my father would retaliate with the little rhyme:

The rain it raineth on the just
and on the unjust fella,
But it raineth more upon the just
For the unjust hath the just's umbrella.

And it's true. Not only do bad things happen to good people, but the effects of those bad things can be so much worse for those whose meagre resources have already been drained by the demands of a grasping world. So Mr Just gets wet not only because it's raining on him, but because Mr Unjust has got his brolly. We might call it 'adding insult to injury'.

When I translate this into the language of world events I see far more serious repercussions of Mr Unjust's selfish habits. I notice, to my shame, that some of the 'umbrellas' that have gone 'walkabout' have my fingerprints on them. The umbrella of the ozone layer, for example, reminds me that my unnecessary car journeys have damaged everyone's climate and caused weather disasters on the other side of the globe. The umbrella of 'consumer choice' reminds me that my expectation of cheap and varied food in every season has been satisfied at the expense of third world economies for whom almost nothing is available at any season.

It is our hands that are holding umbrellas that might have sheltered the world's poorest people from the effects of natural disasters, but have, instead, made these disasters worse.

Yet there are people who turn this tendency to self-interest right over on its head. One such was the elderly uncle of a friend of mine. He was a doctor in a small German town in the 1930s. The people trusted and respected him and he cared for their needs and healed their hurts. But he was Jewish. As the shadow of fascism fell across the village, he was transported to an extermination camp.

Miraculously, he survived, to experience the liberation of the camp where all his family had been murdered.

An old man now, he made his way back to his home village, where he quietly resumed his medical practice.

'Why?' his friends asked him. 'Why would you ever choose to come back here?'

'Because the people need a doctor,' was the simple reply.

Thought for the day

To be fair is merely human; to be just is divine.

Prayer

Lord,
teach us the difference
between our demand for a fair deal
and your Dream of a just world.

Amen.

Oliver McTernan
Second week of Lent

Second Sunday of Lent

A step into the unknown

Gn 12: 1-4; Ps 32; 2 Ti 1: 8-10; Mt 17: 1-19

The Lord said to Abram, 'Leave your country, your family and your father's house, for the land I will show you.'

(Genesis 12: 1)

In a world marred by religious conflicts and staggering inequalities between rich and poor we desperately need icons of hope – people whose lives take us beyond the immediate and who reassure us that things do not have to be this way, that life can be different.

Abraham is a perfect example. Jews, Christians and Muslims hold him in high esteem because of his unconditional response to God's call. He was willing to uproot himself, to leave behind the familiar, and to journey into the unknown, simply because he trusted the God who promised that there was more to life than what he saw around him.

Abraham's future had been secured from the day of his birth. His family lived in Ur, a city at the very hub of life, renowned in those days for its learning and commerce. His father had established a profitable business selling idols. It was in Abraham's own interest to uphold the traditional beliefs and values of the civilization into which he was born. He had everything to lose by questioning the status quo and abandoning the security of his family and city. And yet, excited by God's promise that 'by you all the families of the earth shall bless themselves', he set out to discover what those words could mean.

Lent offers us the opportunity to rediscover the sense of promise and excitement that faith should bring to our lives. It is the time for us to realize that, whoever we are and whatever our circumstances, each one of us shares the call of Abraham. Each one of us has the potential to bring blessings to 'all the families of the earth'. We will only be able to realize this vocation if, like Abraham, we are prepared to question the values of the society into which we have been born and to make ourselves vulnerable in pursuing our belief that life can be different both for ourselves and the millions whose lives are blighted and disfigured by poverty and violence.

Thought for the day
Yes, life can be different if we are prepared to take the risk and to work for change.

Prayer
Lord God,
grant me the courage
to place my trust in the promise that you made to Abraham.
Help me to see beyond the immediate
and not to be imprisoned by the values and ambitions of today's society.
May I never abandon the hope that life can be different.
Whatever the personal cost,
may I always be willing to work to help others
to achieve their full human potential.
Amen.

Second Monday of Lent

A world in need of compassion

Dn 9: 4-10; Ps 78; Lk 6: 36-8

'We have sinned, we have done wrong, we have acted wickedly, we have betrayed your commandments and rulings and turned away from them.'

(Daniel 9: 5)

Although biblical scholars might argue over the date and circumstances in which the Book of Daniel was written, no one doubts that its message reaches beyond time and place. The prophet's sharp reminder that 'We have not obeyed your servants the prophets, who spoke in your name to our kings, our princes, our fathers, and all the people of the land' is as fresh and relevant today as it was on the day it was first written.

The prophets spoke out against the inequalities that existed in their own day, and challenged their contemporaries to be just, fair and compassionate towards the poor and vulnerable. They did not allow them to make the excuse that the poor were responsible for their own plight.

The findings of a global survey published recently by *The Economist* show that there are more rich people in the world today than ever before. And the gap between rich and poor is getting larger. In Britain income inequality has reached its widest level in 40 years. While some worry incessantly about how to manage their money, millions of others worry about how to manage without money.

The prophets understood this to be as much a spiritual as a social or political problem. They did not suffer from the mental dualism that allows us to separate our spiritual life, our prayer and worship, from our everyday life of work or bringing up a family. Worship for them was soulless if did not reflect a willingness to embrace those in need.

Lent is not a time just to test our willpower. Fasting and giving up pleasures during Lent will be futile unless these acts of self denial help us to identify more closely with the plight of the millions who have no alternative but to fast everyday.

'Be compassionate, as your Father is compassionate', Jesus told his followers.

Lent is our opportunity to release the power of God's compassion into a world that stands in much need of it.

Thought for the day

Be compassionate towards everyone whom you encounter this day.

Prayer

God of compassion and forgiveness
empower us this day
to resist the need to judge or to condemn anyone.
Make us generous in mind and heart.
May we always be alert to the needs of others,
and ready to reach out to those in need
whatever their circumstances.
Amen.

Only God can make us agents of change

Is 1: 10, 16-20; Ps 49; Mt 23: 1-12

Listen you heavens; earth, attend,
for Yahweh is speaking.

(Isaiah 1: 2)

When we think about the scale of the injustices and dysfunction of life today and the extraordinary diversity of people's needs it is very easy to think, How can I possibly change things?

Whenever I feel inadequate or unworthy I am always encouraged when I think about the people whom God singled out to achieve what seemed to them to be impossible tasks.

Isaiah is a good example. His immediate response to God's call was to protest that God had got it wrong. He felt totally out of his depth at the thought of being a prophet, the mouthpiece of God. 'I am a man of unclean lips, living among a people of unclean lips,' he declared. It was only when he realized that far from being asked to go it alone he was being invited to work in partnership with God that he felt up to the task.

At baptism we were anointed to continue the work of Prophets like Isaiah. God singled us out to be his mouthpiece and partner in today's world. We can only hope to fulfil our God-given task and become agents of real change in so far as we are ready to allow God to transform our lives. Yahweh's words to his people, 'Though your sins be like scarlet, they may become white as snow; though they be crimson red, they may be white as wool' apply as much to us as to those for whom they were first written.

Lent is our opportunity to recognize and to act upon the persistent need for self-transformation.

Thought for the day

'Do not follow their example. Their words are bold, but their deeds are few.'

Prayer

Lord,
may we never be tempted to use our shortcomings
to excuse ourselves from working to transform our world.
May our words and actions
bear witness to our faith and trust in you.
May we be instruments of your peace and forgiveness
in whatever circumstances we may find ourselves today
and always.

Amen.

Second Wednesday of Lent

The real measure of success

Jr 18: 18-20; Ps 30; Mt 20: 17-28

'Promise that these two sons of mine may sit one at your right hand and the other at your left in your kingdom.'

(Matthew 20: 21)

There is something very human about Matthew's story of the mother who was anxious to secure a good position for her boys, James and John. What parent doesn't want to see his or her child succeed? It is not surprising then that Jesus wasn't perturbed by her request. He simply used this naked display of ambition to communicate what true success involves. 'Can you drink of the cup I am to drink of?' he asked.

The cup in biblical times was symbolic of one's fate. To drink from the same cup as someone else displayed a willingness to share fully in that person's destiny. It wasn't by chance that Matthew records this encounter immediately after Jesus predicted his own public execution. This point would not have gone unnoticed by his readers. To be successful on Jesus' terms simply means being ready to give oneself entirely to the service of others, even at the risk of being publicly humiliated: 'They will turn him over ... to be made sport of and flogged.'

The Eucharist is the moment when this becomes our story. Jesus invites us to share the same cup from which he himself drank. To accept his invitation has consequences for the way we chose to live our lives. In taking communion we express our own willingness to share the fate of Jesus. We commit ourselves to a life of service whatever the personal cost.

Lent is a time for some honest reflection; a time when we should not be afraid to ask ourselves how ready are we to stand up for our beliefs and values even when it may mean being subjected to the public ridicule and rejection that both Jeremiah and Jesus had to endure.

Thought for the day
Am I willing to pay the price of success even if it means nothing less than the sacrifice of my own life?

Prayer
Loving God,
give me the courage to drink from the cup that you offer us in the Eucharist.
May I always be ready to stand up for what is right and just.
Help me to overcome the fear of public ridicule and rejection.
May I never fail to witness publicly to the values that your Son Jesus taught us.
Amen.

Second Thursday of Lent

Are we prepared to speak out?

Jr 17: 5-10; Ps 1; Lk 16: 19-31

'There was a rich man who used to dress in purple and fine linen and feast magnificently every day. And at his gate there used to lie a poor man called Lazarus, covered with sores, who longed to fill himself with what fell from the rich man's table.'

(Luke 16: 19)

The last decade of the twentieth century was probably the most exuberant period of wealth creation in human history. It produced an unprecedented number of wealthy people. At the same time millions of our fellow human beings are suffering hunger and dying prematurely.

In a very real sense there is a contemporary ring to today's Gospel story about Lazarus and the rich man. The gap between the rich and the poor seems to becoming more and more insurmountable.

What does it take to convince people that the present situation is intolerable, and should not be allowed to continue? Should we accept Abraham's pessimistic prediction, reported by Luke, that 'if they do not listen to Moses and the prophets, they will not be convinced even if one should rise from the dead'? Or should we continue to strive for a radical change in the way we live our lives today?

Jer miah got the reputation of being a party pooper because people didn't take warmly to what he had to say. We can understand this reaction when we read the words, 'Cursed is the man who trusts in human beings, who seeks his strength in flesh, whose heart turns away from the Lord.' Few of us take kindly to being confronted so directly. And yet in baptism we have been anointed – which simply means, singled out – to continue the work of prophets like Jeremiah. Are we prepared to run the risk of being cut off, and to lose friends because of our willingness to speak out against today's inequalities and injustices?

Am I aware of what is happening on my own neighbourhood, or am I so caught up in my own affairs, like the rich man's five brothers, that I fail to notice people in need even on my own doorstep?

Thought for the day
Is the gap between me and others insurmountable?
If so, why?

Prayer
Lord God,
help us to listen attentively to the words spoken by the Prophets.
May we never knowingly be indifferent and insensitive to the needs of those around us.
Give us the courage to recognize and to act upon our responsibility for the needy.
May you always find in us a heart generous enough to share our own good fortune with those in need.

Amen.

We are the earth's trustees

Gn 37: 3-4, 12-13, 17-28; Ps 104; Mt 21: 33-43, 45-46

'Here comes the dreamer,' they said to one another. 'Come on, let us kill him now and throw him down one of the storage-wells.'

(Genesis 37: 20)

Joseph's brothers were motivated by a very common human feeling – Envy. They resented the fact that as the youngest Joseph was their father's favourite. They allowed their jealousy and resentment to get the better of them, and they sold Joseph into slavery. They knew well what they were doing, and they were collectively culpable for their actions.

In assessing the morality of our actions, moral philosophers sometimes make a distinction between what they call vincible and invincible ignorance. Sometimes we can find ourselves acting out of ignorance simply because we never made the effort to find out the facts, which we could have done had we wanted. When we act like this we are morally accountable for what we do, and cannot claim our ignorance as an excuse to justify our actions. It is only in situations when it would have been reasonably impossible for us to ascertain the full facts that our ignorance could be described as invincible, and our actions could therefore be said to be free from moral fault.

In highly developed Western societies, which offer us instant media coverage and easy access to all kinds of information, few of us can excuse our actions or, perhaps even more apt, our inaction on the grounds of invincible ignorance.

Today's Gospel reminds us that the earth belongs to God and we are its trustees. We are accountable to God, therefore, for what happens and for how we use the earth's resources. We are our brothers' keepers and God expects us to behave more responsibly than Israel's sons did towards their brother Joseph. And yet, how easy it is for us to turn a blind eye to what is happening both to people and to the earth. We often choose to live our lives only on a need-to-know basis for fear that knowledge and awareness may require us to act differently.

Thought for the day
The greater knowledge we have, the greater also is our moral responsibility.

Prayer
Creator God,
you have entrusted this wonderful world to us
to take care of, and to share in its fruits.
Forgive us for the times we have been indifferent to
the plight of those who, like Joseph,
have been sold into slavery.
May we never be tempted to use ignorance to excuse
our inaction.
May you always find us ready to fulfil our
responsibilities
whatever our circumstances.

Amen.

Second Saturday of Lent

The prodigal son

Mi 7: 14-15, 18-20; Ps 102; Lk 15: 1-3, 11-32

'While he was still a long way off, his father saw him and was moved with pity. He ran to the boy, clasped him in his arms and kissed him.'

(Luke 15: 20)

The concept of unconditional love, a love that is totally independent of our performance, is difficult for most of us to grasp. Why? Because we so seldom experience it in the course of our lives.

The love we receive from partners, parents, priests and teachers often depends on our ability to keep up to their impossible expectations: to always be cheerful, young, beautiful, etc. And the same is true of the love that we give to others. If they become ill, or ugly, or boring, our love is withdrawn.

In today's reading from Luke's Gospel we are given an insight into what it is to be loved unconditionally. The younger son in the story was totally responsible for his own downfall. When he decided to return home he was motivated by feelings of self-pity and self-preservation rather than by any sense of sorrow for what he had done. The father allowed none of this to get in the way of his desire to re-admit his wayward son into the family circle. At the risk of looking foolish in the eyes of the rest of his household, he runs to greet his son. There is no wagging finger or prolonged interrogation, no 'I hope you learnt your lesson'.

The returned prodigal does not have to prove his readiness to change, to perform and to pull his weight this time round before he regains his father's trust. The ring, the sandals, the cloak, are the signs of his restored dignity and status. Their reconciliation is immediate and unconditional.

The story is about God's love for us, a love that we should try to reflect in all our human relationships. God's is a love that allows us space to make mistakes, a love that is not possessive, jealous, or intrusive. That does not mean that God is indifferent to our plight. Whatever our human condition, be it be self-induced through ignorance or arrogance, we remain loveable in the eyes of a God who is always ready to embrace us unconditionally.

So we have no excuses not to respond to God's invitation. No one can claim that he or she is wired up wrongly or has wayward genes that get in the way of a meaningful relationship with God. To quote the words of Helder Camara, if we fall a thousand times, we have to get up for the one thousand and first time.

Thought for the day
The unconditional nature of God's love leaves no room for complacency in our relationship with God, or for indifference in our relationships with others.

Prayer
O God of the prodigal,
protect us from those feelings of unworthiness
that prevent us from recognizing that we are always
loveable and trustworthy in your eyes.
Protect us also from those self-righteous attitudes
that allow us to stand in judgement of those who fail to
meet up to our standards or expectations.
Give us the courage to be loved and to love
unconditionally.

Amen.

Jayne Hoose
Third week of Lent

Third Sunday of Lent

Beyond Culture

Ex 17: 3-7; Ps 94; Rm 5: 1-2, 5-8; Jn 4: 5-42

'You are a Jew and I am a Samaritan woman. How can you ask me for a drink?'

(John 4: 9)

In Christ's meeting with the Samaritan woman at the well we see how he reveals himself to another individual and how her perceptions of him change. The woman must initially have regarded this stranger with a great deal of suspicion. Here was a Jewish man behaving in a way that was far from culturally acceptable. After all, he surely can not have failed to notice that he was associating publicly with a woman, and a Samaritan women at that. Jews did not associate with Samaritans and men certainly did not engage in public conversation with women. Equally, Jesus's disciples, arriving upon this scene, must have been shocked by his behaviour. They seem to have dealt with it in a typically human manner. Let's not talk about it. It'll go away!

However, in Christ's interaction with this woman at the well, he not only lays aside cultural expectations to engage with her as an individual, but reveals himself in a way which it is difficult to find paralleled elsewhere in the gospels. He gradually reveals himself not as a suspicious and perhaps threatening Jewish stranger, and not just as a prophet, but as the Messiah. Christ shows an astounding amount of openness in an interaction that others would regard as inappropriate, yet that he has deliberately initiated.

The way we interact with others reveals something about us. It affects their perceptions of us and probably of others like us. Each and every interaction, every day of our lives, is an opportunity for openness and compassion. Whenever we engage with others it is an opportunity to show them the respect and love they deserve as brothers and sisters in Christ. In a world where our friendships and associations are inevitably affected by cultural considerations ranging from gender, race and education to dress code, accent and age, we are called as Christians to look beyond these, to challenge stereotypes and expectations. Each meeting with another person is an opportunity to be a witness to the Lord's presence through our openness, love and compassion.

Thought for the day
Am I bound by cultural expectations and perceptions or do others see in me the presence of God's love and a faith which builds a spirit of openness and truth?

Prayer
Lord,
strengthened by faith,
open my heart to others,
regardless of their age, gender, faith or nationality.
Give me the courage to meet each person
in a spirit of openness and compassion.

Amen

Third Monday of Lent

What do we value?

2 K 5: 1-15; Ps 41; Lk 4: 24-30

'Send out your light and your truth;
they shall be my guide.'

(Psalm 43: 3)

In Kings 5 we find Naaman suffering from leprosy, a socially and physically debilitating disease which would most likely prove fatal. It is therefore surprising that when Elisha tells him how he can be cured he reacts with anger and not gratitude.

This reaction becomes more understandable when we look at the circumstances that lead Naaman to ask for Elisha's help.

Naaman is an army commander of some standing in an influential land where he has both great wealth and status. Of course Naaman is angry. Suddenly the status and wealth which is so important to him cannot meet his needs. He finds himself in a position where he not only has to rely on his servant to find him healing, but has to turn to a strange prophet from a less important and influential people for that healing. Imagine then how he must have felt when, having swallowed his pride to ask for help, he finds that the process of his cure does not meet his expectations. In fact, it requires him to further challenge his views about the superiority of his own land. How could the resources for his healing come from a lesser nation?

Are we any different today? Is there not something of a similar struggle being played out between the economically rich countries of the North and the economically poor countries of the South? Do we in the North seriously regard the economically poor South as our equal and as being in a position to assist our development and healing? After all, we live in a world where what is valued most highly is money and material wealth, so naturally we imagine that because our economy is larger we are superior to poorer countries.

As Christians we need to break free from these constraints, to face the hard task of using very different values to measure our importance, and to be open to learn from and receive from everyone. We need to engage with others in an atmosphere of mutual respect, which will allow mutual healing and flourishing.

Thought for the day

Do any of the value systems we support prevent us being in solidarity with others?

Prayer

God of all,
guide us on a path which frees us from constraining value systems.
Help us to grow in this freedom
and to meet the challenges for change it may bring.

Amen.

The value of being human

Dn 3: 25, 34-43; Ps 24; Mt 18: 21-35

'Direct me in your ways, Yahweh,
and teach me your paths.'

(Psalm 24: 4)

The parable of the unmerciful servant reminds us that the Christian life is not about keeping a checklist of past failings and debts. The way in which we treat our brothers and sisters is not about calculating whether or not they deserve the love and the compassion we are able to show. Christian love is not there to be earned. It is the right of every individual simply because they are created in God's image.

We could never earn the love that Christ showed us on the cross and, in learning to accept that love, we acquire the ability to give as well as to receive. So the way the servant who is forgiven his debts and yet demands payment from his debtor behaves is unacceptable. In spite of this, we continue build global systems obsessed with counting the cost and assessing worth.

In 1999 whilst in Livingstone, Zambia, I met a small toddler called Maggie. Maggie was an AIDS orphan being cared for by relatives. She was undernourished and suffering from the effects of AIDS herself. Neither the drugs nor the food needed if Maggie was to be properly treated were available. Zambia is required to make large debt repayments; as a result it is unable to meet the basic health needs of its people. The price that is paid is the lives of children like Maggie.

Some progress has been made on the forgiveness of international debt. As Christians we must continue to ensure that the intrinsic value of the person is always put first. Unjust and unforgiving systems should be challenged not just on a global level but also in our everyday lives, by the way in which we free each other as individuals from our debts of past failings to respect the dignity and value of others as children of God.

Let us put aside the energy-consuming and time-wasting process of assessing whether or not particular individuals or groups deserve our respect and love. As they are all children of God, the answer will always be Yes.

Thought for the day
Simply to be human is to be worthy of love.

Prayer
Loving God,
free those trapped by injustice
and help us to respect the dignity of all your children.

Amen.

Third Wednesday of Lent

Trust in love alone

Dt 4: 1, 5-9; Ps 147; Mt 5: 17-19

*'Do not think I have come to abolish the Law
or the prophets: I have not come to abolish them
but to fulfill them.'*

(Matthew 5: 17)

Christ declares in Matthew not an opposition to the earlier teaching of the prophets but a fresh commitment to it. A commitment that requires its fulfilment beyond that called for by the Pharisees and the teachers of the Law. A commitment that insists upon the recognition of the spirit of the Law. This means a move away from a purely legalistic approach to one that focuses upon love. It is a call to a higher level of moral maturity, that moves beyond obedience to the letter of the law to a way of living that accepts God's will for us, and accepting the responsibilities that this brings.

Here we are faced with one of the more difficult teachings of Jesus. Throughout the Sermon on the Mount, of which this is a part, he calls for a change in our basic attitudes, a change so profound that it requires us even to love our enemies. We are challenged, when faced with unimaginable atrocities like those of Auschwitz, Cambodia or Rwanda, not only to pray for and show love and compassion to their victims but also to the perpetrators. In this we find one of the great paradoxes of Christianity. Our enemies inflict great injustices upon us and upon those we love.

The logic of this world would seem to indicate that we should hate them and yet Christ calls us to love them. The transformations required of our enemies will only come about through love. Such is the Kingdom of God.

In the struggle for justice in this world it is hard for us to put our trust in prayer and love alone. Supporting 'good causes' and campaigning for justice are proven ways of making a difference. But they cannot be substituted for love and prayer. They belong together. Meeting our enemies with love has a profound impact, as was shown by the impact made when a father who had held his daughter whilst she died in the Enniskillen bombing in Northern Ireland called a few days later, not for retaliation, but for forgiveness.

Thought for the day
Am I prepared to seriously contemplate the challenge of trusting in love alone?

Prayer
Lord,
teach me to trust in love
and guard me from hatred and doubt.

Amen.

Third Thursday of Lent

Listening

Jr 7: 23-28; Ps 94; Lk 11: 14-23

'Today, if you hear his voice do not harden your hearts.'

(Psalm 94: 8)

The readings today all incorporate the theme of listening and being heard. When Jesus frees the man possessed by the demon in Luke's gospel he allows his voice to be heard. So often we see the effect of evil silencing the voices of individuals and communities. Those who are marginalised in today's society often struggle to find a voice. As when Christ drove out the demon from the mute so we must reject evil in order to hear the voice of God and of others.

In turning away from what is wrong, we must recognise that what we will hear may be unexpected and difficult to deal with. To really open our hearts, and listen to God and to others means avoiding re-interpreting what is said so as to make it fall in line with what we would like to hear.

On the face of it, to be asked to be a listening people seems straightforward, but it can at times be a difficult path to tread. It may require us to put aside our own wants and step beyond the security of frequently trodden paths. It may even require us to move in directions previously avoided and to abandon long-held viewpoints.

We can only reject evil and walk in God's ways when we listen to his will for us and are prepared to be an integral part of a learning community where all voices are heard and respected. Really listening is an essential part of learning from each other and drawing closer to God. In order to serve others we must first listen. Being given the freedom to speak and to be heard, to listen and to learn, is part of the joy of being a Christian family. A genuine search for the true path means a constant and open dialogue, involving not just a privileged few but the whole community.

Thought for the day

Silence is not always golden. It may mean others have no voice or that we are not listening.

Prayer

Lord,
give us discerning and listening hearts
ever open to your voice and to the voice of others.
Having heard the voice of truth
give us the courage to walk the path it requires.

Amen.

Third Friday of Lent

Maintaining a balance

Hos 14: 2-10; Ps 80; Mk 12: 8-34

'Love the Lord your God with all your heart and with all your soul and with all your mind and with all your strength ... and love your neighbour as yourself.'

(Mark 12: 30-31)

This quote from Mark is very familiar to all Christians. These are after all identified by Jesus as the most important commandments. They clearly place love at the heart of the Kingdom of God but they also speak to us of balance, a need to achieve a harmony between looking inward and looking outward. We first need to look towards God with all our being because it is only in knowing something of God that we can know something of what it is to love and to be loved.

In working at our relationship with God and getting to know him better we also learn to recognise the importance and the sheer joy of the fact that we are created in his image. It follows that it is important that we work at getting to know, accept and love ourselves. This is something we can so easily neglect. It can be so much easier to be busy focusing on others and doing as much as possible. As God's commandment tells us, we must also take time to stop and to look inwards. If we are 'to love our neighbour as ourself' then it is only in developing a genuine love of self that we can express real love for our neighbour. If we fail to take this seriously we are in danger of simply being busy fulfilling our need to be needed.

In the absence of taking time to look inward as well as outward we can easily become too intense about our role and lose sight of the joy of Christian ministry. This can lead to an anxiety and seriousness which prevents us truly walking alongside others and recognising that we are merely a tiny fragment in God's plan. We are not solely responsible for taking care of the whole of creation. Keeping a balance between looking inward and outward helps us to recognise that the care of creation may just possibly be within God's grasp.

We can stop trying to conquer the world before breakfast and spend more time simply loving God, self and others, just being – being close to God, being ourselves and being with others.

Thought for the day
Learning to be is about learning the fullness of love.

Prayer
Lord,
help me not to be so busy looking outward
that I forget to take time to stop and look inward.
In learning to love myself
help me to develop a great love for others
so that, in doing so, I might recognise how great your love is.
Amen.

Humility born out of love

Hos 5: 15 - 6: 6; Ps 50; Lk 18: 9-14

'For everyone who exalts himself will be humbled, and he who humbles himself will be exalted.'

(Luke 18: 14)

How many of us read the parable of the Pharisee and the tax collector and react by thinking of the Pharisee, 'What a strange way to pray, I would not pray in that way.' A little more subtle perhaps, but still a thinly veiled reaction not so unlike the Pharisee's own dismissive judgement, 'I'm not like this tax collector here.'

It is often said that the essence of humility is truth. The tax collector recognises the truth of his own state before God. The truth of our situation is often more like that of the Pharisee. Our lack of humility is revealed by the fact that we do not acknowledge this truth, even to ourselves.

How many of us, at first reading, stop to wonder why the Pharisee feels the need to pray in this way? It can at times be easier to simply judge the actions of others rather than look at what may drive those actions. To act towards others out of love often requires us to look beyond the obvious. What is it that compels the Pharisee to compare himself favourably to tax collector before God? A more loving response to this parable might be to try to understand the underlying needs and hurt of both the Pharisee and the tax collector.

It is only when we regard others out of love that true humility follows. Love and humility are essential partners. From self love and acceptance arises the ability to put aside the need for both self promotion and the false humility of self abasement. Love of others allows us to build relationships on acceptance rather than criticism and comparison. Such love allows us to walk alongside each other. To achieve true humility therefore we should put love at the centre of our lives. If we focus on being humble and striving for humility, on the other hand, then we may achieve quite the opposite affect.

Thought for the day

To strive only for humility is to lose sight of the goal. Love and humility are essential partners. True humility is borne out of love and the essence of humility is truth.

Prayer

God,
give us the courage
to both seek and accept the truth,
that we may grow in love and humility.

Amen.

Joseph Donders
Fourth week of Lent

Fourth Sunday of Lent

On Blindness and Seeing

1 Sa 16: 1,6-7; Ps 22; Ep 5: 8-14; Jn 9: 1-41

'Who are you to teach us?'

(John 9: 1-41)

Rembert Weakland, the Benedictine Archbishop of Milwaukee in the United States, wrote some years ago a column in his diocesan weekly, *The Catholic Herald*. He asked himself whether he would be able to find a parallel to the story of the cure of the man blind from birth, rejected by the religious leaders of his day, who had replied, when he told them about his cure by Jesus, 'Who are you to teach us?'.

Weakland explained that the first readers of the gospel would have interpreted this story in their own way. He recognised that the gospel would be particularly meaningful to those catechumens who were preparing to be baptized at Easter, and who might well have been rejected by their family and friends.

But, Weakland asked himself, what meaning might the story of the rejected healed blind man have for me, and for us?

He looked for a parallel in his life, and he found one. Aware of the misery of so many in our world, he wrote:

'If you talk about the disparity between the rich and the poor at home and around the world, if you are concerned about the sanctity of human life everywhere on this globe, if you say that the system is to serve the person and not vice-versa, if you affirm the need to respect the property and goods of others, if you say that the capitalist system leaves many people out in the cold, you are simply dismissed as irrelevant. "Who are you to teach us? ..." I have come to accept that sometimes it is more Christian to be naïve than to have all the answers to the world's problems according to the world's criteria. Let them dismiss me if they will. I simply must go on thinking that what Jesus said was light.'

It is a parallel many Christians could apply to their lives. We might not have all the the answers to the problems of our world, but not closing our eyes to them is the first step our society needs.

Thought for the day
Once I was blind and now I see!

Prayer
Lord Jesus,
give me the courage
to ask you to lend me your eyes
to see the world in which I live,
and to lend me your ears
to hear the cries addressed to you.
Amen.

Fourth Monday of Lent

The New City

Is 65: 17-25; Ps 29; Jn 4: 43-54

'Be joyful, be glad for ever
at what I am creating,
for look, I am creating Jerusalem to be "Joy"
and my people to be "Gladness".'

(Isaiah 65: 17-21)

It is one of the oldest human dreams. It is the oldest vision in Sacred Scripture. There will be a new city, Jerusalem, called 'Joy' and a new people, called 'Gladness'. It is the restoration of the world. In Jewish folklore it is called 'tikkun olam', the repair of the world. With the psalmist people have been praying all through the ages, 'God restore us! Bring us back! Let your face shine on us!' (Psalm 80: 3, 7 and 19).

It is the restoration Abraham and Sarah began to foresee when they left their country and began to walk humanity's pilgrimage towards 'the new eternal city that God had planned and built' (Hebrews 11: 10).

It certainly sounds like a dream: 'I am creating a Jerusalem, full of happy people. I will celebrate with Jerusalem and its entire people. No more will the sound of weeping or the sound of cries be heard in her; in her, no more will be found the infant living a few days only, or the senior citizen not living to the end of his days' (Isaiah 65: 18-20).

They were not the only ones to foresee it. All through humanity's difficulties and battles, prophets, in so many human traditions, kept that dream alive. In the old Central American Indian Mayan tradition, one prayed of old: 'That we all may rise up, that we all may be called, that there be no different peoples among us, and that no one stays behind the rest.'

In the Bible prophets began to foretell that one day Yahweh would intervene: 'Someone would be sent to proclaim the Good News and to begin the healing of the world' (Isaiah 61: 1-2).

That someone arrived when Jesus came among us, beginning the restoration, assuring its success by his death and resurrection, and engaging us in the process. It will be a world, or a heavenly city, where there will be no first, second, third, and fourth world any more. A world that will be without first ones, and without last ones.

It is Jesus' dream. It is our mission.

Thought for the day

Let us walk on, sometimes falling, getting up, brushing ourselves off, reminding ourselves of our goal, and taking another step towards it.

Prayer

My Lord and my Brother Jesus,
keep me hoping,
and help me to find the support and company I need to keep me moving.
Be with me and with all those engaged in the mission you left us,
'to gather into one the scattered children of God'
(Jo 11: 52).

Amen.

Fourth Tuesday of Lent

His Priority

Ez 47: 1-9, 12; Ps 45; Jn 5: 1-3; 5-16

'It was because he did things like this on the Sabbath that they began to persecute Jesus.'

(John 5: 1-3, 5-16)

It was a Sabbath day at the Pool of Siloam. A sick man had been waiting for a cure at the pool of Siloam for 38 years. Jesus took a pity on him, and asked whether he wanted to be healed. Of course he wanted to be healed. So Jesus cured him, and told him to take up his stretcher and walk home.

The authorities blamed Jesus for healing on a Sabbath. They did not tell him that directly. They accused Jesus indirectly. They blamed the healed man, who had done what Jesus had told him to do after his healing: 'Pick up your stretcher and walk.'

That is all he was doing when some representatives of the established order met him. Though it was the first time for nearly forty years he had been able to walk anywhere, they blamed him for carrying his stretcher home on a Sabbath day. They did not like it that Jesus took people, the human person, as his priority, not the Law.

Jesus objected to their list of priorities. Jesus put – in the name of God – a sick man and a woman bent-down by osteoporosis above their interpretation of the law and of God's will.

Today many venerate economic growth statistics, gross national production figures, and other economic indicators above people. It is the bottom line that counts, money is the sacred cow to which human beings are sacrificed.

How many have heard over the years, 'I'm sorry, but it is no longer makes economic sense to keep you employed, or to keep your factory open. We can have the same work done in another country for a lower salary, or we can import the things you produce much cheaper.'

Jesus' priorities are different. For him, development can only mean investment in people and communities. It should do so for us.

Thought for the day

'The question of bread for myself is a material question; the question of bread for my neighbour is a spiritual question' (Nikolai Berdyaev).

Prayer

Lord Jesus
help those in authority share in your concern for the human person
and help all of us to support them in their care for all.

Amen.

Fourth Wednesday of Lent

Feet and Hands

Is 49: 8-15; Ps 144; Jn 5: 17-30

'My Father goes on working, and so do I.'

(John 5: 17-30)

Over the years CAFOD has had partnerships with all kinds of people from all over the world. In those contacts people tell their stories. One particularly beautiful story is told about a Christian Community in Peru, in the parish of Santiago de Pupuja.

The parish council decided to prepare a set of drawings for the Lenten season. A committee was formed. The young people got involved, and the work began. A set of eight scenes was made and they were – to the surprise of many – full of feet and hands. One showed a tree full of fruits with three hands. There was a large painting of the 'New Jerusalem' with four feet. There was one that showed a cross surrounded by five hands and a big foot, and one showing a transfigured Jesus standing on a big foot.

When asked about all those feet and hands, the explanation was simple. They said, 'As Christians we are on our way.'

That is why their main symbols were feet to emphasize the migrant or pilgrim character of a community on its way, and hands to indicate the work that has still to be done. On all of the eight scenes there was only one written text: 'La Alegria y Dios en el Camino' ('The Joy and God on Our Way').

We are on our way! It is a lesson John's Gospel teaches again and again. Jesus is still at work in us and in our world. Like a new website, we are still 'under construction'. The work is not yet over, the pilgrimage is not yet ended.

Before Jesus left them, Jesus told his disciples that he had still much to tell them, but he was not going to do it, because they were not ready to understand it. He promised them that he would send his Holy Spirit, and with the help of his Spirit we would be able to do greater things than even he would have been able to do in his day and age (John 14: 12).

It means that we will have to use our hands and feet!

Thought for the day
Blessed be my feet and my hands, that I may continue to walk your way, doing your work!

Prayer
Lord Jesus,
guide me in the work I do
and on the path I walk.
Help me to understand that I am needed by you
right where I am now,
whatever the future might bring.

Amen.

Fourth Thursday of Lent
Gold and God

Ex 32: 7-14; Ps 105; Jn 5: 31-47

'I know you too well:
you have no love of God in you.'

(John 5: 42)

Jesus' statement, 'You have no love of God in you,' sounds very harsh. Today's readings combine this uncomfortable saying with a reading from the book of Exodus. It is the time when Moses is with God on the mountain of Sinai. God asks him to hurry down, telling him that the people he had led out of Egypt had left the way God had marked out for them, and were making fools of themselves, dancing and worshipping around an idol, the statue of a bull cast in gold. When Moses returned to the camp, he saw them dancing around the gold they had made their idol. They had no love of God left in them.

Before considering the possibility of drawing a parallel with our own time, let us have a look at some history. In his *Annals of Discovery*, Christopher Columbus used the word 'gold' 139 times and the words 'Our Lord' or 'God' 51 times. By January 1493 he had found sufficient gold to be sure of a welcome in Spain. Almost everything seemed to have focused on gold. As the conquest continued, indigenous people were forced into slavery in the search for more and more gold. In 1519 Hernan Cortes took about 2000 lb of gold from Montezuma in Mexico, and in 1531 Francisco Pizarro took about 13,000 lb from the Incas in Peru.

Only the faintest echoes of the old Mosaic divine warnings against idolatry were heard. God and God's people hardly counted or did not count at all – only gold mattered. The effects were disastrous, not only for the indigenous populations of the Americas, but also, in the long run, for the gold adorers themselves.

It is a story that never ends. The worship of gold continues, always at the expense of human sacrifice. It pollutes the air, it spoils the water, it destroys vegetation, it upsets human relations, and it makes people forget about God. Jesus put it bluntly: 'You cannot worship gold and God at the same time' (Matthew 6: 24; Luke 16: 13), while Paul wrote to his disciple and friend Timothy, 'The love of money is the root of all evil' (1 Timothy 6: 10), not condemning the use of money but the worship of it.

Thought for the day

'The fountains are with the rich, but they are no better than a stagnant pool till they flow in streams to the labouring people' (Marguerite Blessington, 1789-1849).

Prayer

Lord Jesus,
lover of all your sisters and brothers,
inspire us to work for human progress,
for peace and justice,
for the integrity of creation,
seeking the spread of your kingdom in all we do.

Amen.

Fourth Friday of Lent

Tested

Wi 2: 1, 12-22; Ps 33; Jn 7: 1, 2, 10, 25-30

*'Let us test him with cruelty and with torture,
and thus explore this gentleness of his.'*

(Wisdom 2: 1, 12-22)

The book of Wisdom describes what would happen to the Servant of Yahweh who would come to restore the world to God's Kingdom, a reign of justice and peace. The prophecy proved insightful. This was precisely how Jesus' opponents taunted him while he was dying on the cross, 'Show us now that what you said is true; let your God save you now....'

They tested him, and according to their lights, he failed. Once he had died, they went home laughing and mocking him, convinced that he had died ignominiously. His gentleness, God's gentleness, did not pay in this world, they thought. They had won. During Lent we are preparing ourselves to celebrate a very different outcome.

The two endings to the story are still played out today. Jesus told his followers that what happened to him would happen to them too. And the arguments reported in the Book of Wisdom are repeated even more confidently today. They were heard in El Salvador when Archbishop Oscar Romero gave a voice to the poor. But listen to how that gentle man responded in his final sermon, preached only minutes before he was shot dead while celebrating Mass in a hospital chapel:

'Let there be no animosity in our hearts. Let the Eucharist, this call to reconciliation with God and our brothers and sisters, leave the imprint of Christianity in all our hearts... Let us pray for the conversion of those who struck us ... of those who sacrilegiously dare touch the tabernacle. Let us pray to the Lord for forgiveness and for the due repentance of those who turned this town into a prison and a torture chamber. Let the Lord touch their hearts. Before the terrible sentence is accomplished – "he that kills by the sword will die by the sword". Let them truly repent and have the satisfaction of looking on him they have pierced. And may there rain from there a torrent of mercy and kindness, so we all may feel ourselves to be brothers and sisters.'

Thought for the day
'To live one's idealism brings with it hazards'
(Martin Luther King).

Prayer
Lord Jesus,
you are not only my example and my model,
you are more than that.
Your life is the one I live.
As Saint Paul once wrote:
'Yet I live, no longer I, but Christ lives in me'
(Galatians 2: 20).
Help me to face the consequences.

Amen.

Fourth Saturday of Lent

Human Rights

Jr 11: 18-20; Ps 7; Jn 7: 40-52

'But surely the Law does not allow us to pass judgement on someone without giving them a hearing and discovering what he is doing?'

(John 7: 51)

Nicodemus made this remark when the police, sent out to arrest Jesus, had come back without taking him in. When asked by their angry chiefs why they had returned empty-handed, they answered, 'There has never been anyone who has spoken as he did.'

When the authorities scolded them for being taken in by Jesus, Nicodemus spoke up. He reminded them to respect the rights of Jesus. He was laughed at, and accused of being led astray, and asked whether he was also from Galilee.

Yet Nicodemus was right. He was a predecessor of those who plead with and pressurise governments and judges to respect the human rights of every citizen. The same right Nicodemus spoke up for was later to be included in the 1948 Universal Declaration of Human Rights:

'Everyone has the right to recognition everywhere as a person before the law.'

Pope John Paul II has valiantly defended the rights Nicodemus stood for. He added a reason for his conviction. In receiving our human life each of us shares in God's breath, breathed in all of us from our beginning. Again and again he repeats in his encyclicals, 'The human being is the way of the Church.'

So many conferences of bishops all over the world have stated the same truth. The bishops of Chile explained in 1985 why:

'....not only because [those rights] are laid down in the Universal Declaration of the United Nations. Our commitment is prior: we believe they are written in the human heart and that Jesus has ratified them more deeply by promulgating the law of love. It is out of our faith in Jesus that we defend human rights...'.

It is good to be actively concerned about the abuses of human rights in far-off countries, but we should not lose sight of the unjust treatment of those close to us, in our parishes or our places of work. And even closer to home, we should not only think of the behaviour of others. In our own judgments and behaviour too we should be aware of Nicodemus' words.

Thought for the day
'If you don't find God in the very next person you meet, it is a waste of time looking for God further' (Mahatma Gandhi).

Prayer
Lord Jesus,
help me not to jump to conclusions about others.
Lead me to respect them for what they are.
Help me to grow in appreciation for their rights,
and help them to respect mine.

Amen.

Jeanne Hinton
Fifth week of Lent

Fifth Sunday of Lent

The master of time

Ez 37: 12-14; Ps.129; Rm 8: 8-11; Jn 11: 1-45

'Yet when he heard that Lazarus was ill, he stayed where he was for two more days.'

(John 11: 6)

I was away from home when I heard a friend I loved was dying. Frequent telephone calls kept me in touch, but could not allay my anxiety to be there in person. A message is sent to Jesus to tell him a friend he loved is dying. 'Come, quick,' is its import. There are so few references in the gospels to Jesus' particular love for an individual; Lazarus is one of those few. Unaccountably, Jesus delays his departure. What is going on here? I find this incident extraordinary and compelling. Twice now during Lent I have stopped reading at this point and 'waited' these two days. The time drags.

This story of the raising of Lazarus is pivotal to what happens next. It is the event that brings Jesus back to Judea from a 'safe place', and on his return he compounds the danger he is in by a deliberately provocative act: the raising of Lazarus, obviously a person of some significance, so close to Jerusalem is likely to raise a storm. Now Lazarus too becomes a wanted person. For Jesus this event is not just about his friend dying; it will bring matters to a climax. So at this point he takes control of the speed at which events will happen. The pace begins to slow down.

There is so much emotion to this story. Manipulation, anxiety, misunderstanding, disbelief, weeping, taunting. Emotions that tear at the gut. How did Jesus manage to stay open emotionally at a time when he was almost certainly facing death himself? In a poignant scene in the well known 'soap', Coronation Street, when facing death from cancer one of the characters quotes a 60s song, 'How hard it is to die/ when the birds are singing'. Jesus too would have felt life burgeoning all around him; springtime in Palestine. How hard then to court death. What sustained him ?

In the classic booklet, *The Master of Time*, Max Warren suggests that it was just this – the personal quality of Jesus' living – that sustained him. That and the way that he handled time. 'The greater the pressure of Time, the more urgent the employment of it, the more distinctly does Jesus act as if Time were of no very great moment,' he writes.

Thought for the day
How do I respond under pressure? What helps? How do I handle time? Is there a rhythm and a pace that is best for me ?

Prayer
Loving One,
help me to find a pace
that gives energy
for the long haul
and the essential tasks.
Amen.

Fifth Monday of Lent

A different future

Dn 13: 1-9, 15-17, 19-30, 33-62; Ps 22; Jn 8: 1-11

A pack of dogs surrounds me,
a gang of villains closing in on me.

(Psalm 22: 16)

We sat opposite each other on a long train journey and she told me her story. Appearances are so often deceptive. It seemed she had so much – she was well to do and her husband was influential – and yet the truth was much more complex than that; painful in the telling.

Our lives were very different, but in hearing her story I was drawn close. Later she made a remark, almost absent-mindedly, shockingly abusive, racist. Taken aback, I couldn't look at her. Instinctively I looked away and down at the floor. Normally I would have reacted, perhaps angrily countering what was said. But now I looked away in consternation. I knew too much about her; some other response was called for. Later pondering this incident, I remembered how Jesus once had looked away, his eyes cast down to the ground. Did he I wonder feel just such consternation ?

Some men drag a woman into the temple court and publicly accuse her. They aren't really concerned about her one way or the other; she is an excuse for their action. What must it have felt like encircled by these angry and abusive men? They had deliberately 'made her stand before them all'. Perhaps just such abuse is all she had ever known. Jesus will have no part in this. His eyes are turned away from her and from her accusers. Did he know these men or know something about them? Unnerved, they certainly thought he did.

'A gang of villains [is] closing in me ...' says the Psalmist. Jesus well knew what it was like to be the focus of an angry and abusive crowd, stones at the ready. He could empathise with the woman from personal experience, but Jesus' empathy goes further than that. He seems to know what it would be like for her as a woman, all those eyes upon her. He did not look up until all her accusers had gone. His affirmation of her as a person of worth offered a different future. His action offered this possibility not only to her, but to her accusers as well.

Thought for the day
What incidents do you know of people who have offered hope to the other by the way they have responded to abuse or worse? How did they do this? What results from an opposite approach where the situation is compounded by each side's refusal to meet the other?

Prayer
Just One,
help us
create more understanding
not less
in our debating
and in our acting.
Amen.

Fifth Tuesday of Lent

A sense of self

Nu 21: 4-9; Ps 101; Jn 8: 21-30

So they said to him, 'Who are you?'

(John 8: 25)

'How do you look into the eyes of Jesus or the Buddha?'

The question is put by the Jesuit priest, Daniel Berrigan, to the well-known Buddhist Zen master, Thich Nhat Hanh. It is not a matter of *how*, but *who looks*, comes the answer:

'It depends on the nature and the substance of the one who looks ... There are those who look into the eyes of the Buddha, into the eyes of Jesus, but who are not capable of seeing the Buddha or Jesus.'

In the encounter with the Pharisees described in today's gospel, Jesus tells them, 'If you do not believe that I am He, you will die in your sins.' If we cannot recognise goodness for what it is, it is bad news for us. There are certain moments in life that concentrate the mind or trouble the conscience: an accident or illness or a deep emotion stirred. Sometimes words can have the same effect, particularly if spoken by someone we respect. Those Jesus was speaking to probably thought their death a long way off, as most of us do. Still, death is the ultimate uncertainty; we might think, it is best to hedge our bets. 'You will die in your sins.' Slung in an angry brawl these words could be disregarded; spoken authoritatively by a good man, some at least must have been disconcerted.

Jesus is not here addressing individuals, but a group – the scribes and Pharisees. At other times he has been specific about their sins – burdening the poor, making themselves rich at the expense of others, practising a false religion and failing to live in the truth – justice, mercy and good faith. It is likely that the worst sins humankind have experienced have been perpetrated in the name of 'the group'. 'Be careful, you are losing your sense of self,' Jung said to a young friend caught up in the euphoria that accompanied the rise of Adolf Hitler.

In the burning anger expressed against the sins of a group, Jesus holds up a mirror to any of us caught in a similar situation. Some of those he spoke to that day looked into his eyes and recognised truth. Each of them rediscovered his or her self. 'It depends on the nature and substance of the one who looks.'

Thought for the day

Have we had an experience of being so caught up in 'the group' that we lost our sense of self? What helped us maintain a sense of self?

Prayer

Dear One
be a mirror for all those
caught up in situations too big or too complex
for them to see the wood for the trees.
May they rediscover who they are.

Amen

Finding the truth

Dn 3: 14-20, 24-25, 28, 52-56; Jn 8: 31-42

*'You will know the truth
and the truth will make you free.'*

(John 8: 32)

I was given the task of writing down the story of the community I belonged to. I got my tape recorder out and started interviewing people. It was not long before I realised there were many different versions of the same story. I could just about pin down the dates, but for the rest I would have to interpret the different versions as best I could. There were many 'truths' to choose from. It gave me a new appreciation for the fact we have four 'tellers' of Jesus' story. The experience also raised for me questions about truth and what it is.

'What is truth?' Pilate later asks Jesus. Jesus gives no answer to that, but at another time he had said, 'I am the truth.' Truth is personal. Bishop Samuel Ruiz of Mexico understands this. An academic, he was considered an unlikely choice as bishop for the remote mountainous area of Chiapas, Mexico's most southerly state. Soon after his appointment as Bishop of San Christobel he undertook a journey by mule, visiting every town and village of his diocese. At first he said he 'was like a fish that sleeps with its eyes open. I travelled through villages where the bosses were scourging debt-slaves who did not want to work for more than eight hours a day, and all I saw were old churches and old women praying. "Such good people" I said, and did not notice that these good people were victims of cruel oppression.'

The goodness he saw in the people moved him to want to know them better. He began to stay in their shacks instead of the houses of the bosses. This brought him close to the people and he saw then for himself the poverty and abandonment in which the indigenous lived. The truth he saw brought an uncomfortable freedom. It changed him into 'a venturesome David prepared to do battle with church and state', like the three young men from today's reading in Daniel.

We cannot find out the truth just from reading a newspaper – we will become informed perhaps, but that is not always enough. To find out the truth we have to come close to people, particularly to those different from us.

Thought for the day

What experiences have you had of your perception being changed by meeting someone different from yourself. How did this feel? What happened as a result?

Prayer

Seeking One
give me a hunger
to know the truth
and an openness to seek it
in those I meet
each day.
Amen.

Care-fronting

Gn 17: 3-9; Ps 104; Jn 8: 51-59

'In all truth I tell you,
whoever keeps my word
will never see death.'

(John 8: 51)

Jesus never seemed to have any problem 'telling it straight'. I am one of those people who rarely can; confrontation being a problem for me. I therefore find myself cringing at Jesus' confrontational style in these passages in John's gospel.

Bible reflection often has this inconvenient way of facing us with a place where we are vulnerable ourselves. Perhaps Jesus never spoke these words – some commentaries tell us that these passages reflect extreme tensions between church and synagogue at the end of the first century. Jesus was certainly good at what David Augsburger, a Mennonite pastor, calls 'care-fronting'.

Speaking on the phone to a friend I went all round the houses, avoiding the issue we needed to talk about. He cut through my flannel with one sharp sentence. Instead of being affronted, I could feel the gratitude flooding through me. We could work the matter out now. The word 'care-fronting' describes Jesus' style of relating with others; uniting love and power. He 'unifies concern for relationship with concern for goals'. To do this effectively 'is to offer the maximum of useful information with the minimum of threat and stress'.

We react to situations of conflict in different ways: I'll give in to make things comfortable; I know I'm right and I'll stick to it; I'll try and find a way to meet you half way, or, Conflict is normal, we can work through this. You might recognise yourself in one of those ways of reacting to a conflict or disagreement. Our personality will determine to some extent which style we feel most comfortable with, but we can learn from experience and change in how we deal with difficult situations.

Jesus' care-fronting exposes, provokes, challenges and also affirms. I know I cannot avoid conflict, and there always seem to be plenty of opportunities to practice skills in responding with patience and respect for the other.

Thought for the day

Think of the last time you were in a situation of conflict. How did you respond? What did you learn from it?

Prayer

Peacemaker
strengthen me to care
and to stand up for what is right,
to appreciate the gifts I have
to help resolve conflict,
and to be open to learn new skills.
Amen.

The journey of growth

Jer 20: 10-13; Ps 17; Jn 10: 31-42

'Is it not written in your Law:
I said, you are gods?'

(John 10: 35)

'Though you are only a man, you claim to be God', they had scoffed. It was one of those telling slips, because in scoffing they demeaned themselves. Jesus' reply takes one's breath away. He reminded them that they too have been called 'gods' – and rightly so. Intent on finding a reason to arrest him, they cannot hear what he has to say. Indeed this truth is strangely hard to hear. Hard because it is an invitation to grow, to gradually realise our own god-likeness.

The past ten years or so have been an unsettling time for me. I have been aware of changing, thinking differently – about a lot of things, God included. Was I 'losing' my faith? I have come to learn more about the stages of faith and stages of growth. The writings of mystics such as Teresa of Avila, Evelyn Underhill and Thomas Merton have added further understanding. 'We come to "realize" and "know" ourselves when we are fully actualized as we are meant to be in the designs of God,' Merton wrote. The inner disturbance that keeps us journeying is the norm. The journey of faith is about becoming more fully human, not less.

James Fowler, a pioneer in the field of stages of faith, recognises mature growth as making real and tangible 'the imperatives of absolute love and justice.' He cites as examples Martin Luther King, Mother Teresa of Calcutta, Abraham Heschel and Dietrich Bonhoeffer. But these are only representatives; there are many others, less well known, perhaps individuals known to us personally.

The examples given suggest that the journey of growth will take us into turbulent rather than calm waters, as Psalm 17 illustrates. It is not necessarily the result, but the attempt to make the journey that is important. The writer on mysticism William Johnson comments:

'As we look at the world today, the greatest problem is ... the imperfection of our love, that is to say, our lack of mysticism, and the people who carry the thrust of evolution are the mystics. They are the vanguards, ecstatically pointing towards the future.'

Thought for the day

What stages of growth can you identify in your own faith journey? Who are the people who have influenced you on the journey? Who are the 'wisdom figures' who will encourage you to journey further?

Prayer

Calling One
you encourage me
to be myself,
to become
fully the person
you created me to be
in your likeness.
Thank you!

The power of truth and love

Ez 37: 21-28; Jr 31: 10-13: Jn 11: 45-56

'If we let him go on in this way everyone will believe in him, and the Romans will come and destroy the Holy Place and our nation.'

(John 11: 48)

What a dilemma for those in authority! As if they didn't have enough to contend with, here is a Galilean troublemaker likely to undo all their hard work in maintaining good relations with the Roman army of occupation. That, and the threat he posed to their personal privileges.

It is the same dilemma that is faced by authorities the world over whenever the status quo is threatened by a different kind of power pushing up from below. Few seem to read the writing on the wall in time. Jewish religious leaders wanted to save their nation and their temple; they lost both. The Jesus movement gained in strength.

In Lent 2001 like many others I was following the progress of the Zapatistas in their walk to Mexico city. Mexico's National Liberation Army is made up of indigenous peoples from Chiapas in the south of Mexico, Samuel Ruiz's diocese. He is the one they trust to act as a negotiator. A conveniently forgotten people, they marched for the constitutional recognition of their indigenous rights. They did so non-violently and with considerable flair and style, with songs and poems and colourful dress. Following their progress made more real Jesus' walk to Jerusalem, and brought to mind all the walking done down the centuries for a more just world.

In *The Nonviolent Coming of God* James Douglas, founder of the Ground Zero Community in Washington, USA, writes of Jesus as 'Bar Enasha', the Human One. For him the second coming is 'happening right now' through the action of 'nonviolent revolutionary movements all across the world.' He sees the spirit of the gospel in the movements that are challenging the domination of money and military might, and calling for another way. It is the same sentiment as that of the El Salvadorean bishop and martyr, Oscar Romero, who said before his assassination that if he was killed he would rise again in his people.

The challenge to those who follow Jesus is to live in solidarity with the poor, like Samuel Ruiz and Oscar Romero. Their way is based on faith in the power of truth and love, that meets violence with non-violent direct action, and combines prayer with the loving struggle for justice.

Thought for the day
Why does the media give more coverage to the violent acts of a minority at demonstrations than to the non-violent witness of the majority? How can we ensure our message is not over-shadowed by violence and the threat of violence?

Prayer
Coming One
help me to know
what sort of future you are creating
and what I can do
to help bring about a more just world.

Amen.

Matthew Kukah
Holy week

Passion Sunday

The difference between love and admiration

Is 50: 4-7; Ps 21; Phm 2:6-11; Mt 26: 14 - 27: 66

A large number of men appeared, armed with stones and clubs. They came forward, seized Jesus, and arrested him.

(Matthew 26: 47, 50)

It used to be said that in the days of the Chinese empires, anyone bringing bad news to the king should come to the palace with his coffin.

We refer to the Gospels as 'the good news'. Whatever our idea of 'good news' – the successful delivery of our first child, the return of a loved one, a promotion – being deliberately harmed is the last thing we might expect to happen to the one who brought it. When people travel great distances to bring us good news, do we give them vinegar to drink? But something extraordinary happened when Jesus brought us good news beyond our imagining – the good news of our salvation. His reward was to die in agony on the Cross.

The Passion is a story of love, admiration and betrayal. It seeks to separate the chaff of admiration from the genuine grain of love. There were many who were fascinated by the teachings of Jesus. Many who followed him into Jerusalem were like the people in a crowd catching sight of a celebrity arriving for an opening night, or welcoming home a victorious football team. But there is a difference between *admiring* Jesus and *following* him.

Matthew's account of the Passion eloquently reveals this difference. When Peter stands close to Jesus, he is not afraid of those who have come to arrest Jesus. Though they are armed, he draws his sword. He shows genuine love. He shows courage. But when he acts merely as an admirer, someone willing only to follow Jesus from a safe distance, he says to the servant-girl, 'I do not know Jesus'. His courage fails.

The lesson is clear. Admirers follow Jesus from a distance. They falter at the slightest push – even an idle conversation is enough to expose their weakness. Those who truly love have no fear – even when they are faced with murderers.

Thought for the day
When you see someone in pain, do you simply feel sorry for them? Or do you thank God that you are more fortunate?

Prayer
Lord Jesus
by your Passion
you have shown that there is no suffering outside of the plans of God.
Give me courage
so that I can be a source of light and strength
to those still struggling to understand that their suffering
is part of your plan for their lives.

Amen.

Monday of Holy Week

Three ways of trying to please God

Is 42: 1-7; Ps 26; Jn 12: 1-11

Six days before the Passover, Jesus went to Bethany, where Lazarus was, whom he had raised from the dead. They gave a dinner for him there; Martha waited on them and Lazarus was among those at the table.

(John 12: 1-2)

A disciple once went to his master and asked, 'Is it right for me to smoke while praying?' The master replied, 'No, but you are allowed to pray while smoking.'

We often have difficulties finding God because we tend to look for him in the wrong places. This week our attention is on God's revelation of himself to us. The humiliation that God's son faced should teach us the hard lesson that, more often than not, we do not find God where we expect him to be. An understanding of how inexplicable God's ways are helps us to hold fast to God's promises even when it seems hopeless to do so. It saves us from thinking that suffering is evidence of God's punishment or displeasure with us.

In the Gospel we come face to face with the sharp contrast between God's judgement and ours. The story is seemingly simple and straightforward. The story also presents us with three different ways of looking at Jesus and relating with him. Martha, Mary and Judas seem to come from different angles. In Luke's account we read the story of these two sisters and their contrasting perceptions of hospitality (Luke 10: 38-42). Martha is caring, hard-working and anxious to play the role of a good hostess, ensuring that her guest is comfortable. Mary, on the other hand, is a silent worker, she believes in presence. We are in no position to judge who is right and who is wrong. It seems as if Mary is vindicated in the end.

In John's account in today's reading, we see another aspect of Mary, anointing the feet of Jesus, acting as a generous friend who spares no effort in showing her love. When Judas intervenes, pointing out that the money might have been better spent on the poor, Jesus defends Mary.

If we take this story too literally we may miss the point. It is not so much the particular way we choose to please God that is important, as Judas tries to imply, rather, it is whether we are acting to please God or to please ourselves that matters. It is very much like prayer. Sometimes, we waste time wondering which is the best way to pray. Surprisingly, Jesus indicates that the patient silence of Mary is as pleasing to God as Martha's effort and hard work.

Thought for the day
When you offer a gift or a donation, are you more likely to give what you can easily afford to do without – or are you willing to make a real sacrifice to help those in need?

Prayer
God,
you have shown me that you are everywhere
and in everyone
and that I will find you
if I let you reveal yourself to me.
Open the eyes of my heart
so that I may meet you
in all the events and encounters of my daily life.

Amen.

Tuesday of Holy Week

'Not I, Lord!'

Is 49: 1-6; Ps 70; Jn 13: 21-33, 36-38

Jesus was troubled in spirit and declared, 'I tell you most solemnly, one of you will betray me.'

(John 13: 21)

A meal is usually an expression of joy and communion. Why then does Jesus speak of sorrow at table with his closest friends? Because, as he explains to them, 'One of you is going to betray me.'

Well, this is not an easy message to take. Why would Jesus not directly tell his friends what was in his mind? After all, earlier John tells us that Jesus was able to know what people thought even without being told (John 2: 25). So, why should Jesus be so deliberately evasive? The self-righteous reactions of his friends are instructive. Every one of them is anxious to publicly proclaim their innocence. Matthew's account of this incident is even more interesting. Each Apostle seeks to clear his name, one by one. Each in turn asks Jesus, 'Surely not I, Lord?' When it comes to Judas, he is suddenly tongue-tied, for he says, 'Surely not I, Rabbi?' (Matthew 26: 25).

The significance of all this can not be lost on us. As we have noted earlier this week, the further we are from God, the weaker we are. Others call Jesus 'Lord', but Judas cannot. Already the spirit of God is far from him.

We all seek a level of self-righteousness. We are all anxious not to be misunderstood. Sometimes, the guilty are more anxious than the innocent to clear their names and this anxiety is more often than not a reflection of guilt. We might learn a lesson from the attitude of Jesus during his trial. He was not anxious to assert his will or determined to clear his name. Yet in the end it is his accusers who are revealed to have been guilty.

When Jesus speaks of going away, it is Peter who is most anxious to know where Jesus is heading for, and it is Peter who boldly promises to lay down his life. But as we see later his enthusiasm is not always matched by action. We too are sometimes anxious to proclaim our willingness to please God even before we have sought God's grace without which we can do nothing. Over and over again, we get things the wrong way round.

Thought for the day
Have you ever been wrongly accused of something you did not do? How have you felt when even your best friend has refused to believe your innocence?

Prayer
Thank you, Lord
for not keeping a record of my sins.
Make me aware of my own shortcomings
and more sympathetic to the faults of others.
When I am accused of doing something wrong
rather than rushing to defend myself
may I confess my faults
and re-examine my life.
Amen.

Wednesday of Holy Week

The disciple's tongue

Is 50: 4-9; Ps 68; Mt 26: 14-25

Judas, who was to betray him, asked in his turn, 'Not me Rabbi, surely?' Jesus answered, 'It is you who say it.'

(Matthew 26: 25)

Jesus placed a lot of emphasis on the value of discipleship, the symbiotic relationship that should exist between the disciple and his or her teacher. It is not a master-slave relationship. On the contrary, the relationship should be so closely knitted that the disciple is able to seamlessly carry on where her teacher leaves off.

Examples include the relationship between Samuel and Eli, or between Elija and Elisha. It was through the mouth of the holy man Eli that Samuel was able to decipher that it was the Lord who was calling him (1 Samuel 3: 10). A disciple has to learn to expect that what befalls their master by way of persecution will likely befall them too.

So Jesus explained to his followers that whatever the world would do to him, his disciples should expect to receive the same treatment. When Isaiah says that the Lord has given him 'a disciple's tongue' (Isaiah 50: 4), he means that he has inherited all the courage and faith of his master. Bearing witness to Truth will be his lot – together with all its attendant challenges.

The close relationship between the teacher and the disciple is based on deep trust, love and commitment.

Judas' betrayal shows us that treachery can come from very close quarters. Judas exploited his closeness to Jesus, he misused the trust which this proximity and access had given him. It is amazing that despite knowing that Judas was going to betray him Jesus still gave him a place at his special table.

In the same way, God constantly allows us time to recognise our sin, to seek forgiveness and mercy and to return to him. God never forces us to act against our own will. This is why, when Judas treacherously says, 'Surely not I, Rabbi', Jesus tells him that they are his own words.

Thought for the day

How do you react when you hear that your best friend has sought to destroy your reputation? Do you confront your friend – or do you wait for them to learn a bitter lesson?

Prayer

O God our Father,
you have given us your spirit
so we can always know what is right.
Grant us your mercy
by helping us to seek your face daily.
When we find the truth,
give us the courage to stand for it always.

Amen.

Maundy Thursday

Sharing our Lord's friendship

Ex 12: 1-8, 11-14; Ps 115; 1 Co 11: 23-26; Jn 13: 1-15

He poured water into a basin and began to wash the disciples' feet.

(John 13: 5)

One day, as a veterinary surgeon was on his way home from work, he found a dog which had been run over by a car. One of its legs had been badly fractured as a result of the accident. He took the dog home, nursed it, and it became part and parcel of his household. He became very fond of the dog. Then, one day, the dog vanished. For weeks and months, he looked everywhere and could not find the dog. He was told to forget the dog because now it was well, it may even have returned to its rightful owner. After a long search, the vet gave up and simply thanked God that he had done what he could to save the dog's life. Then, one evening, he was in his study when it began to rain very heavily. He heard a scratching noise on his door. When he opened the door, he saw to his delight his lost dog. Then, as he opened the door wider to let his lost friend in, he discovered that his friend was not alone. Beside him was a dog with a broken leg.

The story reminds us of Andrew taking his brother Simon to Jesus, just as Philip found the Lord and took Nathaniel his friend to him also.

It is not easy for us to understand the significance of what Jesus did at the washing of the feet of his friends. It was instant, and unexpected, hence Peter's outraged protestation: 'You shall never wash my feet!' It was an everyday occurrence in this dry and dusty landscape for servants to wash their masters' feet. As so often, Jesus took this familiar image, and turned it on his head. After the shock, comes the message: 'You call me master and Lord and rightly so. If I then, the Lord and Master, have washed your feet, you must wash each other's feet. I have given you an example...'.

What have we witnessed at the washing of the feet ceremony today? Just a mere reenactment of an historical event – or an urgent realisation of the radical demands that Jesus is making of us? After today's ceremonies, what will happen tomorrow?

Thought for the day

What do you do when you discover a good friend? Do you keep her all to yourself – or do you seek to share her friendship with others?

Prayer

God of infinite goodness,
Thank you for the wonders of my being.
Thank you for making it possible for me to know your love for me.
Help me to learn to share this love with others
so that through me those who do not know you will come to know you.
May those whom I meet today experience you through me.
Amen.

Good Friday

Conscience and the Law

Is 52: 13-53: 12; Ps 30; Heb 4: 14-16, 5: 7-9; Jn 18: 1-19: 42

Pilate came outside to them and said, 'What charge do you bring against this man?'

(John 18: 29)

Again, as in the readings on Passion Sunday, we are confronted with the themes of love, admiration and betrayal.

The consequence of Peter's decision to follow Jesus from a distance is re-enacted. It means that he had a lot of time on his hands. He engages in small talk, finally veering off to warm himself by the fireside, as people do when they have nothing more serious on their minds than gossip. There a house girl recognises Peter as a friend of Jesus. The very fact that even the youngster on duty at the high priest's door knew that Peter was a friend of Jesus tells us how intimate this friendship must have been, how it must have been common knowledge in the towns and villages. In his brusque denial of their relationship we see the terrible cost of the choice Peter has made to put a distance between himself and Jesus. His courage fails him. As Jesus had warned him: 'Cut off from me, you can do nothing' (John 15: 5).

The trial of Jesus brings out a fascinating dimension of human nature. For the crowd, nothing short of the death sentence would do. Yet, according to the Law, they are not allowed to put a man to death. The Romans too are determined to kill Jesus, but also keen on keeping to the law. Both are caught in the dilemma of how to legitimise their hatred. Pilate himself is an admirer of Jesus, but he does not wish to undermine the legitimacy of his authority. The people tell him that if he sets Jesus free, then he is not a friend of Caesar's and, by extension, not fit to rule.

We see in this moving story resonances with the dilemmas we face between distinguishing what is right and what is lawful in the eyes of the state. We see in Pilate's gesture of washing his hands our own reluctance to take responsibility for our actions, to stand out in the crowd to take the risk to be different. When we fail to rise beyond these limitations and to stand for the truth, we become guilty bystanders.

Thought for the day

How do I react when I see a stranger being mugged? How do I react to laws that unjustly discriminate against the unborn, immigrants, or asylum seekers?

Prayer

O God our father,
you have made us your children.
Help me to recognise you in the face of the stranger
and those who are constantly assaulted.
Give me the courage to stand up on the side of the truth.
When I come face to face with injustice,
let me choose truth and justice
without fear or favour.

Amen.

Staying alert

Rm 6: 3-11; Ps 117; Mt 28: 1-10

Towards dawn on the first day of the week Mary of Magdala and the other Mary went to visit the sepulchre.

(Matthew 28: 1)

Tonight, the centre of our celebration is the Word of God and at the same time a summing up of our own lives as Christians.

The many readings from the scriptures, the Baptisms, the renewal of our baptismal promises, all of these bring into focus the reality of our own journey as followers of Jesus. The Church opens herself up to the world by the range of prayers and reflections during our vigil. The moving ceremony of the fire, the lighting of the Easter candle and the passing of the light from candle to candle through the congregation, the expectant waiting for the coming of the Lord, and the singing of the Exsultet ('Rejoice, heavenly powers! Exult, all creation around God's throne! Jesus Christ, our King, is risen! Sound the trumpet of salvation!') – all powerfully sum up the story of the Christian life.

But the concept of a vigil conjures up many other images: uncertainty, sorrow, hope, expectation, faith and love. These concepts create tensions among us. We keep a vigil because we feel sure of what we expect to happen. But we cannot take anything for granted, as we learn from the story of the ten virgins. Keeping vigil must be characterised by mental alertness. If we get sleepy, if we let our lights die out or our oil run down, we might be caught unawares. In a vigil, it is only those who remain faithful and hopeful that will be able to greet the one they are waiting for.

Mary of Magdala is a fascinating personality. She came to the tomb early in the morning, while it was still dark. The day had not yet broken and among traditional societies, where it is believed that witches and evil spirits are abroad at this time, this was considered a dangerous time for a women to be on the road. Mary of Magdala was alone and afraid. She was in mortal danger. But love urged her on and she was rewarded – as we will be if we too overcome our loneliness and fear to keep watch for the coming of our Lord.

Thought for the day

Have you ever been afraid? How do you react – do you seek a cure for the fear or lie low until the object has passed? What makes you fearless – is it your self interest or the wish to help someone?

Prayer

My dear Jesus,
sometimes, my love for my friends fails when they travel or when they die.
From the example of Mary of Magdala,
I learn that I must remain faithful to my friends beyond this life.
Help me to stay faithful to my friends
and to you especially
during the difficult moments of life.
Amen.

Easter Sunday

The basis of our faith

Ac 10: 34, 37-43; Ps 117; Col 3: 1-4; Jn 20: 1-9

Mary of Magdala came running to Simon Peter. 'They have taken the Lord out of the tomb,' she said, 'and we don't know where they have put him.'

(John 20: 2)

In my first year as a priest, I worked as a chaplain in a Catholic Primary school. I used to spend time with the children after Mass, chatting with them and answering their questions. One day one of the children asked me a question:

'I have a friend in my class who tells me that Islam is a better religion than Christianity. He tells me that Mohammed is superior to Jesus. I do not know what to tell him. Father, what is the difference between Mohammed and Jesus?'

I did not know what to say. To buy time, I asked the other children, 'Who can tell us the difference between Mohammed and Jesus?' A small boy raised his hand. 'Father', he said, 'let me tell him.' I nodded. 'We know that Jesus died and rose up after three days. But Mohammed did not rise from the dead. So that is the difference between them.'

I could not have offered a simpler explanation. I remember some years ago *Newsweek* magazine interviewed Mohammed Ali. He was asked what moment of history he would most like to revisit. The great boxing legend replied that he would like to go back to the time when Jesus died, so he could see how he rose from the dead.

Our belief in the resurrection is what separates Christianity from other faiths. It is central to the lives of Christians. As Paul explains, it is the basis of our faith: 'If our hope in Christ has been for this life only, we the most unfortunate of all people' (1 Corinthians 15: 19).

Thought for the day
Do you think about death? What comes into your mind? Is it fear, anxiety, or joy?

Prayer
My dear Jesus,
you have offered me the same challenge that you faced.
You have assured me that my life is only meaningful beyond this if I live well,
giving others my time and love.
By your resurrection, you have changed our lives.
Your resurrection is a guarantee of my own resurrection.
To you, the Father and the Holy Spirit be glory, Alleluia.

Amen.